T0418643

My Sn Words

Consultants

Ashley Bishop, Ed.D.

Sue Bishop, M.E.D.

Publishing Credits

Dona Herweck Rice, *Editor-in-Chief*

Robin Erickson, *Production Director*

Lee Aucoin, *Creative Director*

Sharon Coan, *Project Manager*

Jamey Acosta, *Editor*

Rachelle Cracchiolo, M.A.Ed., *Publisher*

Image Credits

cover zeremski/iStockphoto; p.2 MaxkateUSA/Shutterstock; p.3 paytai/Shutterstock; p.4 zeremski/iStockphoto; p.5 Josef Muellek/Dreamstime; p.6 gertfrik/BigStock; p.7 Serge_Vero/BigStock; p.8 Fotocrisis/Shutterstock; p.9 Lisa F. Young/Shutterstock; p.10 Bronwyn8/iStockphoto; back cove MaxkateUSA/Shutterstock

Teacher Created Materials

5301 Oceanus Drive
Huntington Beach, CA 92649-1030
http://www.tcmpub.com

ISBN 978-1-4333-3983-7

© 2012 Teacher Created Materials, Inc.
Printed in China WAI002

Look at the snake.

Where is the **snake**?

Look at the snowman

Where is the snowman?

Look at the snorkel.

Where is the **sn**orkel?

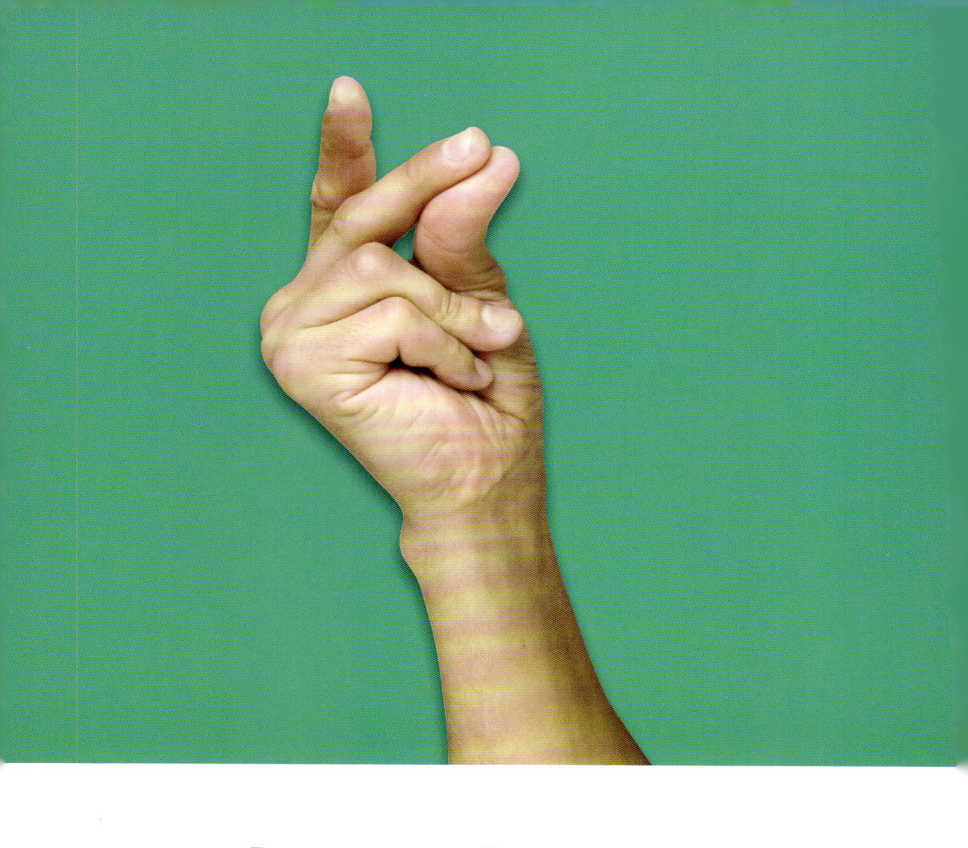

Look at the snap.

Where is the **snap**?

Look at the sneeze.

Glossary

snake

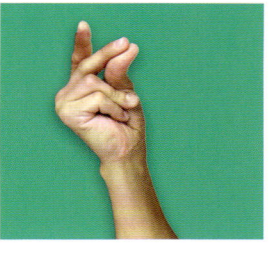
snap

sneeze

snorkel

snowman

Sight Words

Look   at   the   Where   is

Activities

- Read the book aloud to your child, pointing to the *sn* words. Help your child describe where the *sn* objects are found.

- Have your child use toys that snap together to create patterns, build towers, or model numbers.

- Have your child practice sneezing into his or her elbow. Discuss how important it is to wash your hands after sneezing or coughing.

- Have your child say "sssssssnake" while making the letter *s* in the air.

- Help your child think of a personally valuable word to represent the letters *sn*, such as *snack*.